Listen To Me!

Pearce W. Hammond

Listen To Me!

Pearce W. Hammond

Listen To Me!

©2011 Pearce W. Hammond
ISBN-13: 978-1461132790
ISBN-10: 1461132797
LCCN: 2011913752

Inside book design by Pearce W. Hammond
Cover design by Pearce W. Hammond
Cover Dog "Pooh" - Owner Margaret Haithcock
Cover photo by Margaret Haithcock

Published in the United States by
Halftide Publishing
20 Bellinger Cove
Okatie, South Carolina 29909

Contents

FORWARD

Dogs were domesticated from gray wolves about 15,000 years ago. If you had glanced across a campfire back in the Stone Age, you might have seen that dogs looked a lot like those in your neighborhood today.

Dogs may have been the first animal to be domesticated and have been the most widely kept working, hunting, and companion animal in human history. The word "dog"

may also mean the male of the species, as opposed to the word 'bitch" for the female of the species.

Dogs were very valuable to early human settlements as they performed many roles for humans, such as hunting, herding, pulling loads, protection, assisting police and military, companionship, and, more recently aiding handicapped individuals. For example, a German Shepherd guide dog led her blind companion the entire 2100 mile Applachian Trail.

Dogs impact on human society has given them the nickname *"Man's Best Friend"* in the western world.

Man's Best Friend!

We are the one absolutely unselfish friend that you can have in this selfish world. We are the one who never deserts you. We are the one that never proves ungrateful or treacherous. We are the one who will stand by you in prosperity and in poverty, in sickness and in health. We will sleep on the cold ground where the wintry winds blow and the snow drives fiercely, so we can be near your side. We will kiss the hand that has no food to offer and we will lick the wounds and sores that come in encounter with the roughness of the world. We will treat you like a prince even if you are a pauper, and when all other friends desert you, we will remain. When riches fly away and your reputation falls to pieces, we will be as constant in our love as the sun in its journey through the heavens.

*In loving memory of my
Golden Retrievers
Salty, Poppy, Holly, and Lorrie
who touched my life in so many ways
and made this work possible.*

People Question:
Can dogs write poetry and is there a Canine Poets Hall of Fame?

Pooh's Answer:
Do we ever roll in stuff that stinks?

Fireplugs

Oh, what a majestic sight,
standing so proud and tall,
with all of my favorite scents and smells,
sprayed upon its walls.

Many friends before me,
have made their presence known,
so now it's my turn,
to decorate this throne.

So I get into position,
and cock the old back leg,
and in the twinkle of an eye,
I've emptied out my keg.

And when I'm finally finished,
and the last drop hits the sand,
I know whoever sniffs this fireplug,
will know that I'm a man!

P.S. Fireplugs really turn me on
because of all the calling cards
that other dogs leave for me.

Perfuming Your Body

To perfume your body,
go find something dead and rotten,
and roll from head to toe,
roll and roll, and roll and roll,
'til you can't roll no moe.

Then take the smell with you,
and pass quickly through the door,
and look up at your master,
and roll all over the floor.

And when they scream and yell,
and say you smell like hell,
just wag your tail and smile,
and let them delight in your new smell.

This 'tis not shoddy,
'tis the best way to perfume your body!

P.S. I really prefer to roll on top
of dead birds and horse manure.

Bones

Bones, bones everywhere,
and all the yard did shrink,
bones, bones everywhere,
it's hard for me to think.

Some bones are new,
and some are old,
but their taste and smell,
touches my very soul.

So when I die,
please bring me back,
as a clone,
of my favorite bone.

P.S. I go into withdrawal if I can't
find a bone that I've buried.

Cats

Roses are red,
violets are blue,
I hate cats,
and I hope
you hate them too!

P.S. I haven't been able to catch a cat yet but
there are a few in my neighborhood
who have used 8.9 of their 9 lives!

Obedience Training

I bet you'd hollow,
if you had to wear an electric collar.

When they tell me to come,
I ain't dumb,
I've had enough jolts,
from all those volts.

P.S. The shocks are beginning to affect
my sense of smell and it could ruin my sex life!

Collars

*Collars come in all shapes and sizes,
and in all colors including red, white and blue,
but I've never found a collar yet,
that didn't choke the hell out of you.*

*I don't know why I have to wear them,
so tight around my neck,
with all of those stupid tags and licenses,
I'm turning into a wreck.*

*So pull that collar off of me,
and really set me free,
I promise I'll never run away,
just try it and you'll see.*

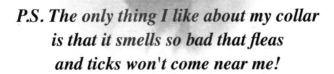

*P.S. The only thing I like about my collar
is that it smells so bad that fleas
and ticks won't come near me!*

Digging

I dig all day and dig all night,
and sometimes miss a meal,
but it makes me mighty proud,
to turn my yard into a mine field.

One of these days,
I'm gonna get me a shirt,
with 4 letters on it,
"GOD, I LOVE DIRT"!

P.S. You would snort, wheeze, and sneeze
yourself if you had 3 pounds of dirt
stuffed up your nose all the time.

Riding In A Car

When I'm riding in a car,
I feel like a movie star,
my head hanging out the window,
taking in every sight,
my ears flapping in the wind,
and flying like a kite.

I smile at a few drivers,
and bark at all the rest,
and cruising in a car,
is what I love to do best!

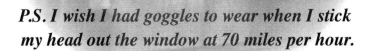

P.S. I wish I had goggles to wear when I stick
my head out the window at 70 miles per hour.

My Nose

My nose can root around in the dirt,
or find a dirty sock or shirt.
My nose can pick up the scent of a garbage can,
or find something rotten to roll on in the sand.
My nose can find a piece of raw meat,
or a cookie, biscuit, or doggie treat.
My nose can point out a dozen Quail,
or detect the mailman bringing the mail.
My nose can smell anything sweet,
or find a bitch in heat.
My nose can smell things smaller than a mouse,
or detect a burglar entering the house.
My nose can smell a car full of drugs,
or a mattress full of bed bugs.
So now I hope that you can see,
what my nose can do for me.

P.S. I can smell a Pizza a mile away.

Garbage Cans

I like to bury my nose in the sand,
but what really turns me on,
is knocking over a garbage can.

Sometimes I even get lucky,
and find a little meat,
and that's an added bonus,
and a very special treat!

P.S. I really like to go through
garbage cans and look for treats.

21

Chew Sticks

If you don't want to make me sick,
don't give me a rubber bone,
or a rawhide chewstick.

Give me something that's easy to chew,
like a pound of sirlion steak,
or a nice T-bone will do.

P.S. If your food budget is really tight,
I'll settle for some raw hamburger meat.

Chasing Your Tail

There's no better sport around,
than chasing after your tail,
you run around in circles,
and wail, and wail, and wail.

You know you'll never catch it,
but it's so much fun to try,
especially when it itches so bad,
that you think you're gonna die.

So when you're old and gray,
and skinny, sick and frail,
I hope you can still run around in circles,
and chase after your tail.

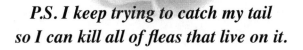

P.S. I keep trying to catch my tail
so I can kill all of fleas that live on it.

Chasing Hubcaps

The thrill of victory,
the agony of defeat,
ripping hubcaps off cars,
speeding down the street.

My father before me,
my uncle and aunt,
they all chased hubcaps,
so don't tell me I can't.

It's really quite a thrill,
to chase after hubcaps and take a spill.

So instead of wasting my time,
looking for some bitch in heat,
I'll keep on chasing hubcaps on cars,
speeding down the street.

P.S. I'm really hooked on this sport
and I'm proud to be called
a hubcap junkie!

24

Garbage Men

From three blocks away,
it's easy for me to tell,
when a garbage man is coming,
it must be the smell.

I might like that man,
if he would just stay away,
from my garbage can.

One of these days,
with a little luck,
I'm going to catch him,
before he reaches his truck.

But until that day comes,
I'll keep barking until he drives away,
and wait patiently for another day.

P.S. Garbage men always make
the hair stand up on my back.

Dog Food

Come here boy,
I've got you a special treat,
but when I rush up to my bowl,
it's the same old mystery meat.

I try to act excited,
but it's getting harder for me to fake,
especially when I see him stuffing down,
a giant sirlion steak.

You know I'm not an average dog,
and I don't like my food served cold,
I'm your best friend and companion,
and I have a heart and soul.

So if you want to make me happy,
and keep me in a good mood,
then throw away all of those cans and bags,
and start feeding me your food!

P.S. I dream about having a super-sized
cheeseburger with french fries.

Swimming Pools

When summer comes,
and the days are hot,
I ain't no fool,
I'm finding me a swimming pool.

And when I find one,
I'm going to swim and dive,
Cause that really makes me feel alive,
And that ain't no jive.

I like to swim in a pool,
and I like to swim in the sea,
but what really turns me on,
is drowning every flea.

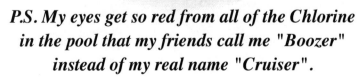

P.S. My eyes get so red from all of the Chlorine
in the pool that my friends call me "Boozer"
instead of my real name "Cruiser".

Flying

I always start crying,
when I know I'll be flying,
They put me in a little box,
and shove me down below,
and when they slam the cargo door,
there ain't no light in there no more.

I'd much rather stay at home,
and be with all my mates,
instead of being crammed inside of a plane,
with all the baggage and the crates.

So the next time that I go flying,
you'll be the one doing all the crying,
instead of sticking me down below,
with all the baggage and the mail,
I'll be up in your First Class seat,
sipping on a cool cocktail!

P.S. I'm tired of being treated like a package
instead of a dog. How would you like to be
drop-shipped by air?

Going To The Vet

If I'm your best friend and pet,
then don't take me to the vet,
I've been going there for over a year,
and they still don't know my name,
and really don't seem to care.

They sample my stool,
with a three foot tool,
and before they examine the smear,
another thermometer is shoved up my rear.

Before you leave me to spend the night,
come check out my room,
it's really out of sight,
It only measures three-by-three,
which makes it impossible for me to pee,
if you don't believe me,
then come inside my room and see.

P.S. They need to call me by my name
instead of a patient number.

29

Duck Hunting

I've never liked breaking the ice,
and freezing at the crack of dawn,
I'd much rather stay at home,
and chew on my favorite bone.

Go get 'um boy, I always hear,
but why should I really care,
I'm not the only one who can float,
why don't they ever jump out of the boat.

So when I get older,
and start to tire,
let me stay at home,
and sleep by the fire.

Maybe one day with a little luck,
I won't have to get up so early,
and go chase after some stupid duck!

P.S. I think all of this started when I retrieved
the paper early one morning in the rain.

30

People Question:
Do dogs have daily thoughts and wisdom?

Pooh's Answer:
Do we ever drink out of the Toilet?

Rolling on dead birds
makes the best perfume!

Never leave home
without your bone!

Cats shouldn't have
8 more lives than dogs!

Food always tastes better
on the floor!

Happiness is a
new chewstick!

Life is empty
without a bone!

See and hear twice as
much as you bark!

Tennis balls are for mouths -
not rackets!

No dog should have to go
through life without sunglasses!

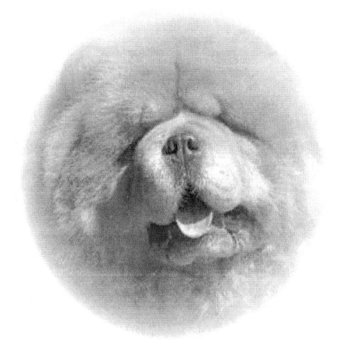

Car windows are for
sticking your head out of!

Smoked pig ears
are gifts from God!

Never Trust a Cat!

When you age 7 times faster than people, you deserve more respect!

Always empty your bladder before leaving a Fireplug!

Sleeping 22 hours a day
doesn't mean
you're brain dead!

True love is a slice of Pizza
you find on the floor!

Relief is spelled
FIREPLUG!

I'd walk a mile
for a Pig ear!

The best perfume comes from
rolling on dead birds!

Be generous . . . give blood
to a tick and shelter to a flea.

Bark when you feel like it!

Consider who will inherit your bones when you die!

"Woofing" is the art of swallowing without tasting!

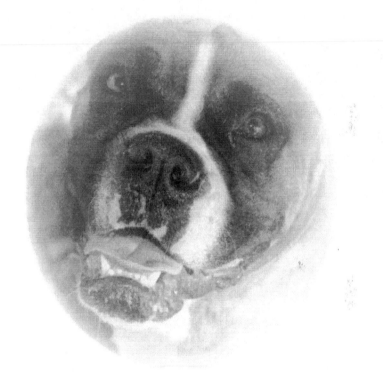

Shrimp breath is never caused from eating shrimp!

Never criticize anyone for chasing their tail!

Bitches and Bones are a winning combination!

Always have clear title
to your back yard!

Never trust your ball
to a stranger!

Always think through your nose!

A bitch in heat is music to my nose!

Mud puddles are the best
grooming parlors.

Always raise your tail in the
company of strangers!

Never bite the hand
that treats you!

Sniffing butts
beats kissing any day!

Living room sofas are more comfortable than the floor!

Every Dog House should have a sofa and Air Conditioning!

Flea collars don't keep all fleas off your rear end!

If your water bowl stays empty for 3 days, you've been mistaken for a Camel!

Barking keeps your
throat muscles in shape!

Noses are for finding
something rotten to roll on!

Brush your teeth
with Chewsticks!

A T-bone steak-a-day
keeps the Vet away!

Cars shouldn't be named
after Cats.

Never wait for your bone
to come in,
go out and dig it up!

Peanut Butter chewsticks would change the world!

Always spin around at least 4 times before eating!

Garbage cans are made
to be turned over!

Garbage man
"Make My Day"!

Getting a driver's license shouldn't be based on the number of legs you have!

57 variety is the spice of life!

The 5 most important words
in any language are . . .
The Pizza Man is Coming!

Pizzas should be eaten
before the kids get home!

Never roll on top of
anything that smells good!

Water taste much better
out of a toilet!

A day without meat
is like a day
without sunshine!

Happiness is keeping
your nose in the dirt!

Never lie down without scratching the ground!

Always leave a *"Big Surprise"* on a lawn when someone is watching!

What stays on the
kitchen counter is yours,
what hits the floor
is mine!

Any pill the Vet gives you
should be buried inside of
a pound of Peanut Butter!

Chasing cars should become an Olympic Event!

A double Cheeseburger a day keeps the Vet away!

Mailmen make the hair
stand up on your back!

Road kill never makes
its own gravy!

Four legs are better than two!

Real Bar-B-Que is a smoked Pig Ear!

People Question:
Do dogs have physical and medical needs?

Pooh's Answer:
Do we ever smell each other's behinds ?

Feeding Us: Feed us at the same time each day. Sometimes we feel like we live in 12 different time zones when it comes to your feeling us! We get so hungry that we chew off all of our nails and then swallow two pounds of linoleum kitchen floor waiting on you to feed us. If you're not going to feed us for a few days, the least you can do is drop some of your food on the floor instead of into that fat human mouth of yours!

Giving Us a Pill: The next time you try to force a pill down our throat, if you haven't coated it with at least a pound of peanut butter, or hidden it inside of a filet mignon, we're going to take your arm off at your elbow!

Grooming Us: Stop yelling at us when we chew our nails and lick and scratch ourself at 3 am. With you bugging us to death all the time, that's the only time during the day that we can groom ourselves. Also, stop telling us how bad we smell. If you were not as tall as the exhaust pipe on your car and your stomach dragged the ground, you would have a hard time staying clean yourself!

Washing Us: I'd rather make friends with a cat than be washed, flipped and dipped. Whatever you use to kill our fleas almost kills us. That's why we always go looking for something rotten to roll on. If you want to start giving us a bath in a bathtub, we promise we'll never roll on top of anything dead and rotten for a week. We'll also stay off of the sofa while you are watching the tube.

Clipping Our Nails: Stop using your nail clippers to clip our nails. Spend a few bucks and get dog nail clippers and make sure you don't cut our nails too short and make them bleed. If you make them bleed one more time, we're going to make the house look like the return of the vampire and we're going to leave surprises everywhere!

Our Shrimp Breath: Stop telling us that we've got shrimp breath and taking us to the Vet to find out what's wrong. Just remember, your breath isn't exactly a bright ray of sunshine, and you know that most of us always have shrimp breath and we're proud of it. We are also real proud of our green teeth.

Our Fleas: Our fleas, like your taxes, are a real pain in the rear end. So, when we wake up in the middle of the night and start scratching and chewing on them, don't get so pissed off at us. You would also scratch and itch your private parts if you had those little b..... all over you.

Our Diet: We're tired of having the same old cheap dog food to eat every night that has no meat in it. How about a nice warm meal every night like the one you have. And, stop believing that we are accommodating animals who will eat whatever you give us. We need some variety in our diet, like a T-bone steak or Filet Mignon, or a nice Sirlion steak right off the grille. We also would not turn down a Pizza or a double Cheeseburger and a large order of fries.

Coughing: You always blame me for waking you up at 3 a.m. with my coughing and then blame me again when you trip over me on your way to the bathroom to take a leak. I have tried unsuccessfully to tell you that my problem is not coughing. My problem is snooring because I have a nose full of dirt from digging and rooting around all day. So wake up and stop trying to force your cough medicine down my throat. If you want to give me some of your medicine, try wrapping an Aspirin inside of 10 pounds of peanut butter or include it as a topping on a large Pizza!

Artificial Respiration: Before doing artificial respiration on me, please check first and make sure that I'm not just relaxing. Remember, I'm no spring chicken anymore, and, when I sleep, you have accused me of being brain dead. You know perfectly well that the hardest thing that I do during the day is follow the sun from room-to-room around the house. Also, I've never been the most alert dog in the world. However, should you observe that I have stopped breathing, then go ahead and give me artificial respiration but remember that the kids will miss me if you don't do it right and something happens to me. If there's an obstruction in my throat, use a coat hanger to get it out. Make sure my tongue is sticking out but don't get too close or my shrimp breath will put you to sleep. Place both hands below my shoulder blade and over my ribs and press down firmly to empty my lungs. Release the pressure so my lungs will fill as the normal elasticity *(I learned that word from the vet)* of my chest returns to its normal position. If my

68

lungs don't fill back up, you are the one who will have to tell the kids!

Docking and Cropping: If you ever try to cut and reshape my ears or shorten my tail, I'll chew up every pair of your shoes. I'll also bark every morning at 3 a.m. and I'll sleep next to your bed when I have bad gas. How would you like it if someone docked and cropped you. Think what your friends and neighbors would say about you!

Destruction: That's a hell of a term to use when your vet talks to you about putting me to sleep when I get old and senile. Remember, you are responsible to care for me in my old age and spare me any unnecessary suffering. Don't let me linger on painfully hoping that I will die soon. Go ahead and pull the plug on me but don't tell the kids that I was destructed!

Low Energy: Whenever I'm on my back in the living room catching a few rays of sun, stop looking at me like I'm in a brain dead trance. And stop rushing me to the vet and telling them that I don't have any energy. The vet then tells you that I have low blood sugar, or something like that, and sells you a bunch of pills for me to take. What I really need for more energy, are several large hamburgers or pizzas three times a day. Also a super-sized order of french fries would be nice.

10 Ways To Protect Dogs From Summer Heat

1. Always make sure that we have plenty of water. Please don't mistake us for a Camel and leave our water bowl empty for three days.

2. If you go out jogging on a hot day, don't take us with you because we can't sweat out body heat like humans and can collapse from a long distance run.

3. Don't walk us in the hot summer sun for long. Walk us early in the morning and in the cool part of the evening.

4. Make sure we have some kind of enclosure with a roof over it when you put us outside. If you do leave us indoors when you go to work, please leave the air-conditioning on for us.

5. Never keep us inside a car with the windows rolled up. The sun may not be on the car when you leave but it can shift quickly. Also, you may think you're going to spend a few minutes away from us, but you may bump into a friend, get delayed in a line, or forget about us and wander off. Remember, windows are for sticking our heads out of.

6. Remember that with hot weather we can also suffer from sunstroke, sun poisoning, sunburns and skin cancer just like you. So, never leave us outside to swelter without shelter for any period of time.

7. If you take us to the beach, put us under your umbrella and put waterproof SPF 15 sunblock on the exposed areas of our skin. Don't bother putting it on our fur because it won't add any protection and we'll probably lick it off.

8. Ask your vet what brand of sunscreen is best because some of us are allergic to certain ingredients. And, if you notice any skin problems, take us to the vet immediately.

9. Hot weather also brings on fleas so please put us on a monthly pill to keep them away. Don't let our bodies become a retirement home for them.

10. In summary, remember that hot weather can kill so take extra care of us during the hot summer months and protect us from the sun and heat.

People Question:
Do dogs have a Bill of Rights?

Pooh's Answer:
Do we have 4 legs?

Bill Of Rights For Dogs

If we like it, it's ours.

If it's in our mouth, it's ours.

If we can take it from you, it's ours.

If we had it a little while ago, it's ours.

If it's ours, it must never appear to be yours in any way.

If we're chewing something up, all the pieces are ours.

If it just looks like ours, it's ours.

If we saw it first, it's ours.

If you are playing with something and put it down, it automatically becomes ours.

If it's broken, it's ours.

People Question:
*Are there any famous
people quotes about dogs?*

Pooh's Answer:
Do we age faster than people?

Let dogs delight to bark and bite,
for God hath made them so.
Issac Watts

I think I have a right to resent
to libelous statements
about my dog.
Franklin Delano Roosevelt

If you pick up a starving dog
and make him prosperous,
he will not bite you.
This is the principal difference
between a dog and a man.
Mark Twain

The more I see of men,
the better I like my dog.
Frederick the Great

If a dog's prayers were answered,
bones would rain from the sky.
Proverb

A good dog deserves a good bone.
Ben Johnson, 1635

No one appreciates the very special genius of
your conversation as a dog does.
Christopher Morley

The best thing about a man is his dog.
French Proverb

Man is a dog's idea of what God should be.
Author unknown

Dogs' lives are too short. Their only fault, really.
Agnes Sligh Turnbull

Dogs are amazing creatures and give unconditional love.
For me they are the role model for being alive.
Gilda Radner

The greatness of a nation and its moral progress can be
judged by the way its animals are treated.
Mahatma Gandhi

If you think dogs can't count, try putting three dog
biscuits in your pocket
and then giving Fido only two of them.
Phil Pastoret

If you get to thinking you're a person of some influence,
try ordering somebody else's dog around.
Will Rogers

I wonder what goes through his mind when he sees us
peeing in his water bowl.
Penny Ward Moser

A dog can express more with his tail in seconds than his
owner can express with his tongue in hours.
Author Unknown

I love a dog. He does nothing for political reasons.
Will Rogers

You think dogs will not be in heaven? I tell you, they will
be there long before any of us.
Robert Louis Stevenson

To his dog, every man is Napoleon; hence the constant
popularity of dogs.
Aldous Huxley

Dogs are not our whole life,
but they make our lives whole.
Roger Caras

The dog is a gentlemen;
I hope to go to his heaven, not man's.
Mark Twain

People Question:
Are there any jokes about dogs?

Pooh's Answer:
Do we ever pee on fireplugs?

How many dogs does it take to screw in a lightbulb?

Golden Retriever: *The sun is shining, the day is young, we've got our whole lives ahead of us, and you're inside worrying about a stupid burned-out light bulb?*

Border Collie: *Just one. And I'll replace any wiring that's not up to code.*

Malamute: *Let the Border collie do it. You can feed me while he's busy.*

Dachshund: *I can't reach the stupid lamp!*

Toy Poodle: *I'll just blow in the Border collie's ear and he'll do it. By the time he finishes rewiring the house, my nails will be dry.*

Rottweiler: *Go Ahead! Make me!*

Shi-tzu: *Puh-leeze, dah-ling. Let the servants. . . .*

Lab: *Oh, me, me!!! Pleeeeeeze let me change the light bulb! Can I? Can I? Huh? Huh? Can I?*

Cocker Spaniel: *Why change it? I can still pee on the carpet in the dark.*

Doberman Pinscher: *While it's dark, I'm going to sleep on the couch.*

Mastiff: *Mastiffs are NOT afraid of the dark.*

Chihuahua: *Yo quiero Taco Bulb.*

Irish Wolfhound: *Can somebody else do it? I've got a hangover.*

Pointer: *I see it, there it is, right there...*

Greyhound: *It isn't moving. Who cares?*

Hound Dog: *ZZZZZZZZZZZZZZZZZZZZZZ*

Australian Shepherd: *Put all the light bulbs in a little circle...*

Old English Sheep Dog: *Light bulb? Light bulb? That thing I just ate was a light bulb?*

"Dogs need to sniff the ground; it's how they keep abreast of current events. The ground is a giant dog newspaper, containing all kinds of late-breaking dog news items, which, if they are especially urgent, are often continued in the next yard."   Dave Barry

81

People Question:
*Are there any interesting
facts about dogs?*

Pooh's Answer:
Do we ever dig holes in yards?

Interesting Facts About Dogs!

* The first search and rescue dog on the scene at the World Trade Center on 9/11/2001 was "Bear", an 11 year old Golden Retriever. He began recovery efforts immediately working 18 hour days in the beginning.

* Rin Tin Tin was the first American dog movie star and signed his own contracts for 22 movies with a paw print.

* According to the Guinnes Book of World Records, the longest lived dog was an Australian Cattle Dog named Bluey who lived to be 29.

* The first living being to travel in space was a small mixed breed dog named Laika. She was sent into space in an artificial earth satellite in 1957 by the Russian Government.

* The only sweat glands a dog has are between the paw pads. The only way they can discharge heat is by panting.

* A dog's sense of smell is one of the keenest in nature. If a pot of stew was cooking on a cooker, a human would smell the stew, while the dog could smell the beef, carrots and all the other ingredients in the stew.

* It was recently discovered that dogs do see in color, just not as vivid as the color that humans see.

* Giving dogs chocolate could be fatal for them because an ingredient of chocolate, Theobromine, stimulates the central nervous system and cardiac muscle.

* Dogs live 15 years on average.

* The top five favorite breeds of dogs in the US are: Labrador Retriever; Golden Retriever; German Shepherd; Beagle; and Dachshund.

* The Doberman breed was created in the 1860's by Louis Doberman, a German tax-collector who created the dog to protect him while he worked.

* Greyhounds can reach a speed up to 45 miles per hour.

* One of the very first animals domesticated by humans was the dog.

* The "spring" in Springer Spaniel referred to this dog's ability to spring or startle game.

* The Poodle haircut was originally meant to improve the dog's swimming abilities as a retriever, with the pom-poms left in place to warm their joints.

* Nearly all but two breeds have pink tongues. The two exceptions are the Chow Chow and the Shar-pei, both with black tongues.

* The first seeing-eye dog was presented to a blind person on April 25, 1938.

* A German Shepherd guide dog led her blind companion the entire 2100 mile Applachian Trail.

* A dog's mouth exerts 50-200 pounds of pressure per square inch.

* A one year old dog is as mature, physically, as a 15 year old human.

* The average city dog lives 3 years longer than a country dog.

* 87% of dog owners say their dog curls up beside them or at their feet while they watch TV.

* Obesity is the #1 health problem among dogs.

* Dog's nose prints are as unique as a human's finger prints and can be used to accurately identify them.

* 70% of people sign their pet's name on greeting and holiday cards. 58% put pets in family and holiday portraits.

* The phrase "raining cats and dogs" originated in 17th century England when it is believed that many cats and dogs drowned during heavy periods of rain.

* Dogs have no sense of time.

* The world's smartest dogs are thought to be (1) the Border Collie; (2) the Poodle; and (3) the Golden Retriever. The dumbest dog is believed to be the Afghan hound.

* George Washington had 36 dogs, all foxhounds, with one named Sweetlips.

* All dogs are identical in anatomy with 321 bones and 42 permanent teeth.

* Female dogs are only ready to mate "in heat" twice a year for a total of roughly 20 days.

* There are 701 types of pure breed dogs.

* An American Animal Hospital Association poll showed that 33 percent of dog owners admit that they talk to their dogs on the phone or leave messages on an answering machine while away.

* Barbara Bush's book about her English Springer Spaniel, Millie's book, was on the bestseller list for 29 weeks. She was the most popular "First Dog" in history.

* Dogs may not have as many taste buds as we do. They have about 1,700 on their tongues while we have about 9,000 but that doesn't mean they're not discriminating eaters. They have over 200 million scent receptors in their noses while we have only 5 million so it's important that their food smells good and tastes good.

* Each day in the US, animal shelters are forced to destroy 30,000 dogs and cats.

* It has been established that people who own pets live longer, have less stress, and have fewer heart attacks.

* Most pet owners (94%) say their pet makes them smile more than once a day.

* Scientists have discovered that dogs can smell the presence of autism in children.

* 'Seizure Alert' dogs can alert their owners up to an hour before the onset of an epileptic seizure.

* The expression "three dog night" originated with the Eskimos and means a very cold night - so cold that you have to bed down with three dogs to keep warm.

People Question:
Are there any dog movies?

Pooh's Answer:
Do we ever stick our heads out of car windows?

Movies About Dogs

Lady and the Tramp - 1955

The Fox and the Hound - 1981

101 Dalmatians (Animated) - 1961

The Incredible Journey - 1963

Oliver and Company - 1988

Eight Below - 2006

Homeward Bound: The Incredible Journey - 1993

Old Yeller - 1957

Bolt - 2008

Iron Will - 1994

White Fang - 1991

Greyfriars Bobby - 1961

Movies About Dogs

The Legend of Lobo - 1962

Savage Sam - 1963

Homeward Bound II: Lost in San Francisco - 1996

A Dog of Flanders - 1999

Air Buddies - 2006

All Dogs Go to Heaven - 1989

Atomic Dog - 1998

Baileys Billion$ - 2005

Beethoven - 1992

Benji - 1974

Best in Show - 2000

Beverly Hills Chihuahua - 2008

Movies About Dogs

Bingo - 1991

Call of the Wild - 1997

Cats & Dogs - 2001

Dog Park - 1999

Iron Will - 1994

Firehouse Dog - 2007

Fluke - 1995

Good Boy - 2003

Hotel For Dogs - 2009

Marley & Me - 2008

Oh Heavenly Dog - 1980

Man's Best Friend - 1993

People Question:
Are there any songs about dogs ?

Pooh's Answer:
Do we ever lick our private parts?

Songs About Dogs

I Wanna Be Your Dog - *The Stooges*

Black Dog - *Led Zeppelin*

Dogs - *Pink Floyd*

Martha My Dear - *The Beatles*

Atomic Dog - *George Clinton*

Hound Dog - *Elvis Presley*

Bird Dog - *The Everly Brothers*

Walking The Dog - *Rufus Thomas*

I Love My Dog - *Cat Stevens*

Chasing Cars - *Snow Patrol*

Ol Egg Sucking Dog - *Johnny Cash*

Old Blue - *The Birds*

People Question:
Can people learn about their health from dogs?

Pooh's Answer:
*Do we ever bark when
we see a letter carrier ?*

Learn About Your Health From Dogs

Naps are essential and should be taken daily.

Enjoy your meals.

Don't think too much.

Drink lots of water .....then slobber it on the floor.

Demand to be petted.

Enjoy nature - the sights, the sounds, the smells . . .

Bark when you feel like it.

Don't let people make you dress up.

Take baths when you're really dirty and then shake yourself dry joyously.

Whine if your needs are not met.

Make friends with everyone in the neighborhood.

Don't go for a run without your ID.

When the people you love come home, make them feel welcome.

Give a lot of kisses - the sloppier, the better.

Chase your tail - who says you can't amuse yourself?

Don't eat food that's too hot.

Stop and smell the roses *(and the grass, trees, fence posts . . .)*.

Wag your tail a lot - it's good exercise for the body and the soul.

Make sure you take plenty of walks.

Everyday should be an adventure.

Never turn down attention.

Never bite the hand that feeds you.

On a nice warm summer's day, stand out in the rain.

Always save room for dessert.

Spend lots of time lying around and staring out the window.

Don't always do what people tell you to do.

Stretch often - with your whole body.

Remember to play!

People Question:
Are any people foods toxic for dogs?

Pooh's Answer:
Do Golden Retrievers like to swim and retrieve things?

People Foods Toxic For Dogs

Some foods which are edible for humans, and even other species of animals, can pose hazards to dogs because of their different metabolism. Some may cause only mild digestive upsets, whereas, others can cause severe illness, and even death.

The following common food items should not be fed to dogs. This list is incomplete and a guide because you cannot possibly list everything that your dog should not eat.

1. Avocado - The leaves, seeds, fruit, and bark contain persin, which can cause vomiting and diarrhea.

2. Bones from fish, poultry, or other meat sources - Can cause obstruction or laceration of the digestive system.

3. Alcoholic beverages - Can cause intoxication, coma, and death.

4. Chocolate, coffee, tea, and other caffeine - Contain caffeine, theobromine, or theophyline, which can cause vomiting and diarrhea and be toxic to the heart and nervous systems.

5. Cat food - Generally too high in protein and fats.

6. Fat trimmings - Can cause pancreatitis.

7. Fish (raw, canned or cooked) - If fed exclusively or in high amounts can result in a thiamine (a B vitamin) deficiency leading to loss of appetite, seizures, and in severe cases, death.

8. Grapes, raisins and currants - Contain an unknown toxin which can damage the kidneys.

9. Macadamia nuts - Contain an unknown toxin which can affect the digestive and nervous systems and muscle.

10. Milk and other dairy products - Some adult dogs may develop diarrhea if given large amounts of dairy products.

11. Mushrooms - Can contain toxins which may affect multiple systems in the body, cause shock, and result in death.

12. Onions and garlic - Contain sulfoxides and disulfides which can damage red blood cells and cause anemia. Garlic is less toxic than onions.

13. Raw eggs - Contain an enzyme called avidin which decreases the absorption of biotin (a B vitamin). This can lead to skin and hair coat problems. Raw eggs may also contain Salmonella.

14. Raw meat - May contain bacteria such as Salmonella and E. coli which can cause vomiting and diarrhea.

15. Salt - If eaten in large quantities, it may lead to electrolyte imbalances.

16. Sugary foods - Can lead to obesity, dental problems, and possibly diabetes mellitus.

17. Table Scraps - In large amounts, table scraps are not nutritionally balanced. They should never be more than 10% of the diet. Fat should be trimmed from meat; bones should not be fed.

18. Yeast dough - Can expand and produce gas in the digestive system, causing pain and possible rupture of the stomach or intestines.

19. Xylitol (artificial sweetener) - Can cause very low blood sugar (hypoglycemia) which can result in vomiting, weakness and collapse. In high doses can cause liver failure.

People Question:
Do dogs age faster than people?

Pooh's Answer:
Do we ever have fleas?

Calculating a Dog's Age

It's common knowledge that dogs age faster than people. But the conventional wisdom that one dog year equals seven human years is an oversimplified view of how old your dog is in human years. The main factors that determine how fast a dog ages and how long it normally lives are:

Size. On average, small dogs have a life span 1.5 times that of large dogs.

Breed. The breed of dog is a strong indicator of life expectancy. Small breeds tend to live longer than large breeds. However, there are a number of exceptions. For example, it is common for a Doberman Pinscher *(a large breed weighing about 77 pounds)* to reach 15 years of age and sometimes 20, whereas the smaller Boxer is shorter-lived and often does not reach 10 years of age.

Gender. Female dogs tend to live longer than males. Depending on breed, the female generally lives one to two years longer on average.

Neutering. On average, neutered dogs live longer than intact dogs. This is largely due to reduced risk of cancer. Research has shown that the sooner the neutering is done, the lower the risk of cancer in later life.

Living conditions. Dogs which are properly feed and kept tend to live longer and be healthier than those that are not. Important factors are: diet, exercise, living conditions and medical attention.

Individual characteristics. Just as some people are born with a strong constitution while others are prone to illness, so are some dogs. Consequently, while one can calculate the expected lifespan of a dog based on the above factors, this is only accurate as an average and individual dogs will vary somewhat from this.

Infancy vs Maturity. Dogs spend a larger percentage of their lives in the adult phase. This is particularly true of smaller breeds and longer lived breeds. A small dog with an expected lifespan of 15 years would be mature, sexually and physically, within one year. A man with an expected lifespan of 75 years would have the same level of maturity at 15 years of age. Because dogs mature at different rates than people, it is inaccurate to say that 1 dog year is equal to so many human years *(e.g. to say that 1 dog year is equal to 7 human years)*. One must take into account the rate of maturity, along with the aging factors discussed above, to obtain an accurate calculation.

The table on the following page matches dog years to human years and takes into account the fact that dogs mature differently than people. It also takes into account the dog size in determining expected lifespan.

Human Years to Dog Years

Human Years	Under 20 lbs Dog Years	20-50 lbs Dog Years	50-90 lbs Dog Years	Over 90 lbs Dog Years
1	15	15	14	12
2	23	24	22	20
3	28	29	29	28
4	32	34	34	35
5	36	38	40	42
6	40	42	45	49
7	44	47	50	56
8	48	51	55	64
9	52	56	61	71
10	56	60	66	78
11	60	65	72	86
12	64	69	77	93
13	68	74	82	101
14	72	78	88	108
15	76	83	93	115
16	80	87	99	123
17	84	92	104	
18	88	96	109	
19	92	101	115	
20	96	105	120	

The oldest recorded age for a dog is 27 human years.

The information above considers the expected lifespan and aging of dogs. In addition to considering how old one's dog will get, it is also important that a dog remain fit and healthy as much of its life as possible.

30 Questions Dogs Want Answered

1. Don't you realize that if you could bark and we could talk that we would both be in a heap of trouble?

2. Why do we always get the urge to lick our paws and groom ourselves at 3 a.m.?

3. Don't you wish you had a tail that you could wave in the air to show how invincible you were?

4. Who said that following the sun around the house all day wasn't hard work?

5. Why can't we taste a steak when we "woof" it down our throats in less than a second?

6. How would you like to get shots each year and then have to wear a license tag around your neck for the rest of your life?

7. Why isn't chasing hubcaps a major sporting event when it has both the thrill of victory and the agony of defeat?

8. Why do you complain about my shrimp breath when the cat smells like it slept in a Sardine can for 3 weeks?

9. Why do you always look at us after you've had beans for supper?

10. Why does furniture taste so much better than chew sticks?

11. Why can't we get a driver's license?

12. Why can't you buy me a pair of sunglasses like yours so I can go outside with you?

13. Why are you having a fence installed? Is it to keep us from getting the garbage man?

14. Why do we have to age faster than you?

15. Why can't you understand why hubcaps have much more pull on us than the full moon?

16. Why do you always tell people that "she's coming in season"? Are we going to Miami Beach?

17. Why do you let our water bowl stay empty for 3 days? Have you seen any humps on our backs lately?

18. Why can't you install a fire hydrant in the bathroom?

19. Why do you think the floor is more comfortable than your bed or sofa?

20. Why can't we have some cats over for a spend the night party?

21. If we are your best friend, constant companion, protector, and hunting buddy, why can't we enjoy a supreme Pizza every once in a while?

22. Why do you wake us up at 4 a.m. to go duck hunting when you know how much the kids like to have us around the house?

23. Why can't we bring you one of your smelly socks at 3 a.m.?

24. Why can't table scraps be a major part of our diet?

25. If cats can bring you dead bird trophies, why can't we come inside the house after we've rolled in something dead and rotten?

26. Why do we always go on automatic pilot when we get within three hundred yards of a bitch in heat?

27. Why can't we get clear title to our front and back yard?

28. Why do cats have 8 more lives than us?

29. Why can't you clone our favorite bone?

30. What's wrong with drinking water out of a toilet?

What Dogs Want From People

Treat us kindly, my beloved friend for no heart in all this world is more grateful for kindness than our loving heart.

Do not break our spirit with a stick for though we should lick your hand between blows, your patience and understanding will more quickly teach us the things you would have us learn.

Speak to us often, for your voice is the world's sweetest music, as you must know by the fierce wagging of our tails, when your footsteps fall upon our waiting ears.

Please take us inside when it's cold and wet for we are a domesticated animal, no longer accustomed to bitter elements.

We ask no greater glory than to have the privilege of sitting at your feet beside the hearth.

Keep our pans filled with water for we cannot tell you when we suffer thirst.

Feed us clean food that we may stay well, to romp and play and do your bidding, to walk by your side, and stand ready, willing and able to protect you with our life, should your life be in danger.

And my friend, when we are old and no longer enjoy good health and sight, do not make heroic efforts to keep us going, as we are not having fun. Please see that us trusting life is taken gently.

We shall leave this earth knowing with the last breath we draw that our fate was always safest in your hands.

About The Author

Pearce W. Hammond is most qualified to write this book. He has been a dog owner and dog lover and has been listening to dogs for over 40 years. He came by his skill for writing quite honestly. His uncle was famed Savannah, Georgia-born songwriter, Johnny Mercer, who wrote over 1,000 songs and won four Academy Awards for *"Moon River"; "Days of Wine and Roses"; "In the Cool, Cool, Cool of the Evening;"* and *"On The Atchison Topeka and the Santa Fe."*

Hammond had an interest in writing at an early age and was encouraged by his uncle Johnny to pursue the craft.

The author is also an accomplished artist whose work has been featured in many local and regional publications. A native of Savannah, Georgia, he and his wife, Anne, reside on the tidal waters and marshes of the Chechessee River in Okatie, South Carolina .

About The Cover Dog - "Pooh"

Pooh is a Springer Spaniel, approximately 7 years old, who has never known a stranger. She enjoys a happy-go-lucky life cruising the banks of Hazzard Creek and visiting with all of her neighbors on Bellinger Cove in Okatie, South Carolina.

Pooh's favorite sport is chasing squirrels *(which she never catches)* and cheering on her sidekick, Boots, *(an older 57-variety black and white female)* at whatever Boots is chasing after but never actively participating with her.

According to Pooh's owner, Margaret Haithcock, Pooh and Boots are "OP Dogs" *(Other Peoples Dogs)* because of the way the two dogs came to live with her: *"One day in January my husband*

Eddie and I came home and there was a bag tied to our front door handle with a note from a neighbor, Terry, whom we had never met, saying that her two dogs had never come home and would we give them their flea and heartworm medications? The next time we heard back from Terry there was a knock on our front door. When Eddie opened the door, Terry stood there with the two dogs and I heard her say, 'I would like to meet the woman who stole my dogs'! Then, before Terry could stop them, both dogs ran inside our house and laid on their dog beds. From that moment on, Pooh and Boots have been our dogs but we still share them with all of our neighbors, including the author of this book."

"OP" Dogs *(Other Peoples Dogs)*
"Pooh" and "Boots"

"Pooh"   **"Boots"**

Other Books

By Pearce W. Hammond

"*The Gullahs of South Carolina*"

This book tells an urgent and important story about the Gullah people of South Carolina and their vanishing way of life and culture. The book is illustrated with the author's paintings and creates public awareness of the unique Gullah language, lifestyle and culture so that future generations will know and recognize the significant contributions the Gullah people have made to South Carolina and to America's heritage.

Paperback   2011   ISBN 9780615486482
Library of Congress Control Number: 2011929319

Available wherever books are sold.
www.pearcehammond.com

Made in the USA
Charleston, SC
13 March 2012